Local
Highwaymen

Clive Whichelow

Published by

Enigma Publishing
4 Charnwood Avenue
London SW19 3EJ
www.enigmapublishing.co.uk

First edition October 2000

ISBN 0 9524297 7 2

By the same author:
Mysterious Wimbledon (with Ruth Murphy) ISBN 0 9524297 0 5
More Mysterious Wimbledon (with Ruth Murphy) ISBN 0 9524297 5 6
Pubs of Wimbledon Village (Past & Present) ISBN 0 9524297 1 3
Secrets of Wimbledon Common & Putney Heath ISBN 0 9524297 6 4
The Local Mystery of Robin Hood ISBN 0 9524297 2 1

Printed by Roebuck Press

CONTENTS

HANDING OVER THE DISPATCHES

INTRODUCTION

The highwayman has held a place in the public imagination ever since he first demanded purses on dark and lonely roads. The roads of Wimbledon, Kingston, Putney, Croydon, Richmond and Wandsworth were all dangerous to travel in the 17th and 18th centuries – the Golden Age of the highwayman. The lonely heaths and the busy coaching routes provided rich pickings for the masked malefactors.

Their methods varied wildly, from the chivalrous and gallant as enshrined in highwayman legend to the vicious, brutal and desperate that was perhaps the more common approach by villains who well understood the folly of compromise.

Whichever method was used the perpetrators usually ended up on the gallows all the same. And some were then displayed on gibbets as a warning to others, as was Jerry Abershaw on Putney Heath.

Looking at biographies of highwaymen who operated locally it is surprising to note the wide area from which they came. Some originated from the north of England, some from Scotland, Wales and even Ireland, and in the case of Claude Duval, from France.

Wherever they were based few of them confined their activities to one area, but to keep one step ahead of the authorities would vary their hunting grounds from Wimbledon Common to Hounslow Heath, and from Richmond to Wandsworth as well as much farther afield. This ringing of the changes may help to explain why even the legendary Dick Turpin appears in local reports for a time.

It is sometimes difficult to separate fact from fiction when writing about highwaymen as their exploits were the stuff of legend almost from the time they took place. Even as these 'gentlemen of the road' awaited their fate in Newgate prison hawkers were selling cheaply printed and lurid tales of their exploits. Then when they were eventually 'turned off', as the charming phrase of the day had it, at Tyburn or some other place of execution the presses would be clattering out yet more biographies. But this book attempts to find out more about the local robbers while laying to rest some of the more outlandish myths and misconceptions surrounding them.

EARLY HIGHWAYMEN

The Golden Age of the highwayman spanned the 17th and 18th centuries but examples of highway robbery can be found as far back as Elizabethan times. Although these incidents lack the scale and style of those of the coaching era they serve to throw into sharp relief the audacious exploits of the larger-than-life characters which followed.

The robberies took place in all local areas such as Wimbledon, Croydon, Putney, Wandsworth and Kingston, but the most notorious area seems to have been Coombe, known in the 16th century as Coombe Park. And the chance of ending up on the nearby gallows at Kingston for so petty a crime as stealing someone's cloak does not seem to have deterred would-be robbers. A few typical examples of early highway robbery follow:

On June 26th 1564 four highwaymen, Hugh Perde, Robert Marshall, John Mason and Matthew Locwood assaulted William Rowdon and John Rowdon at Coombe Park. They stole a tawny-coloured tunic worth 30 shillings, a pair of green hose (17s), a sword (16s), and a purse containing 9 shillings. Marshall and Locwood were further charged with another highway robbery in Reigate and the four were found guilty and sentenced to hang.

In July 1598 two labourers, Christopher Herneman and Thomas Newton were also sentenced to hang for the relatively petty offence of robbing a 30-shilling cloak from William Macham at Coombe Park.

Wimbledon highwaymen seem to have fared better. In July 1591 Roger Straw, a labourer from Wimbledon was found not guilty after being charged with stealing 2s 8d, a cloak and a sword from Geoffrey Cartway in Roehampton. And in February 1595 Wimbledon Yeoman Robert Garroud was found not guilty of stealing a cloak, a rapier, and eight shillings from John Wonham at Coombe Park.

Although many of the highway robberies around this time were committed by labourers, we find in 1577 two tailors, Henry Gossedge of Streatham and Richard Thomas of East Grinstead teaming up with wheelwright Edward Bonsell of Croydon to commit a highway robbery. They assaulted Thomas Barrett in Croydon and stole a tablecloth, seven table-napkins, 6 needlework cushions and a pair of sheets. Only Thomas was found guilty, and he was allowed clergy (a waiving of conviction for a first offence).

What is striking about some of these early highway robberies is that the perpetrators got very little for their trouble. Apart from the occasional purse with a few shillings, they often had to content themselves with stealing their victim's clothes or weapons. But even clothes could be of value if stolen from the right people.

On October 14th 1594 labourer Thomas Smyth attacked Henry Crockford, a servant of John Reede Esq. in Wandsworth and stole two black velvet cloaks, a white satin doublet, a pair of black velvet hose, a black cloth cloak, a grogram doublet, a pair of grogram hose, a pair of silk netherstocks, a black beaver hat, and a girdle (embroidered with silver), and a dagger – all belonging to the servant's master. The value of this haul was given as £60 – a lot of money at the time. Smyth was remanded without sentence due to weak evidence.

In Elizabethan times it was still incumbent upon the local authorities to reimburse people for any losses sustained while travelling. This obligation inspired crafty criminal minds to new tactics. In March 1571 two bakers, John Wyatt and Richard Sturmye were charged with attempting to defraud the inhabitants of Kingston and Elmbridge hundred. On August 10th 1569 Wyatt had bound Sturmye and left him lying on St. George's Hill at Walton-On-Thames. Sturmye claimed to have been attacked by highwaymen and robbed of £11 16s. The story was not believed however, and Wyatt was found guilty. Sturmye somehow managed to escape justice and at the time of the trial was still at large.

This legal loophole was partially closed in 1585 when an act of parliament reduced the obligation of the hundreds to reimburse only half of travellers' losses.

Even by the reign of James I highway robbers were still risking their lives for relatively small returns. In 1605 two labourers, James Ashfeild and John Robertes were hanged for stealing a cloak, two hats, a scarf, sword, pistol and three shillings from Angelo delli Angellii in Kingston. In March 1623 we find four labourers, John Williams, James Fenton, John Sedgsworth and Richard Lane assaulting John Lambe in Croydon and taking £4, a cloak, girdle, hat, gloves, a ruff and a pair of cuffs. For this Sedgsworth was hanged. Lane was not caught, and the other two were already dead by the time of the trial.

So the petty highway robberies went on, the victims losing their purses, cloaks, and sometimes their horses, and the attackers often losing their lives on the gallows, but a new era was soon to come. The coaching age was nigh, and the movement of considerable sums of money and valuables, and the carriage of mail were to provide rich opportunities for highwaymen. By the mid-17th century highwaymen were to become individually infamous and often romantic figures to be enshrined in popular folklore, legend, ballad and literature. The Golden Age of the highwayman was about to begin.

JERRY ABERSHAW

Jerry Abershaw was not even born until the latter part of the highway robbery era but his story is presented first because it is the best documented of all those concerning local highwaymen. He is sometimes described as the 'last of the highwaymen', and while this is not strictly true, he was probably the last of the prominent ones. So much so that his story has almost overshadowed those of all others locally.

Born Louis Jeremiah Avershawe in Kingston in 1773 he had turned to highway robbery by the relatively young age of 17. His parents have been described as 'poor but honest folk', and Jerry's first job too was honest. He was a post-chaise driver.

What attracted him to highway robbery is not recorded but by the age of 17 he was the leader of a gang based at the Baldfaced Stag inn on the old Portsmouth Road.

Despite his youth Abershaw was an uncompromising villain, unlike the dashing highwaymen of legend. One Hounslow innkeeper described Abershaw and his later companion Dick Ferguson as 'terrible, cursing and swearing, and thrusting the muzzles of their pistols into people's mouths'. Though he did concede that this was probably the best demeanour for a successful highway robber.

It is said that Abershaw lived in Coombe Wood and plotted with his gang at the Baldfaced Stag inn. The nearby Portsmouth Road was an ideal place for highway robbery, being as it was the main stagecoach route from London to Portsmouth. On the other side of the Common, what is now Parkside was the stagecoach route from the suburbs into central London. People travelled in constant fear of highwaymen and often put their money in their boots for safekeeping.

Although Abershaw was far removed from the romantic image of the loveable rogues of legend he did possess a healthy sense of humour.

One foul November night Abershaw was taken ill on the Portsmouth Road after an evening of robberies and retired to the Baldfaced Stag. A young doctor, William Roots, was called from Kingston, and bled the patient. Just as the doctor was about to leave Abershaw stopped him and said: 'You had better have someone go back with you as it is a very dark and lonesome journey'.

The doctor however, said he had not the slightest fear, even if he should meet with Abershaw himself. The highwayman very much enjoyed the irony of this and of course the confirmation of his notoriety and was said to have frequently repeated the story with relish. But Abershaw's humour seemed to be at its best when his personal fortunes were at their worst - at the time of his trial and eventual hanging. A classic example of gallows humour.

As highwaymen usually committed their robberies masked it is difficult to attribute specific incidents to individuals, but a glance at contemporary newspaper reports such as those of the Times shows that there was a significant increase in local highway robberies from 1790 – the year that Abershaw began his career. And some of these reports portray someone very like Abershaw. For example, this one from January 7th 1790:

'On Sunday Mr Wells and his wife were going over Putney Common in a single horse chaise when they were stopped by two highwaymen with crapes over their faces who took a gold watch and nine guineas.' The highwaymen were described as being young men who behaved *'very civil'* (it was early days yet!) and were *'exceedingly well-mounted on black horses.'*

Or this one from December 6th the same year:

'Thursday afternoon, between three and four o'clock as Mr Burnell and Mr Platt of Putney were taking an airing on Wimbledon Common in a phaeton, they were stopped by three highwaymen, exceedingly well-mounted, who, presenting pistols to their breasts demanded their money and took from them two gold watches and their purses containing 16 guineas and some silver. They were all young men and wore masks.'

The robberies continued locally over the next five years and the victims included both ordinary travellers and nobility. One incident, from 1793, again has the audacity and ironic humour of Abershaw about it. On March 27th the Times reported that:

'On Monday, at dusk two highwaymen stopped three captains of the militia on Wimbledon Common and robbed them of their purses and watches. After wishing them goodnight they advised them to hasten back to their regiments.'

And so it went on, with Abershaw and his men constituting something of a one-gang crime wave and managing to evade the authorities. When the heat was on Abershaw would retreat to a safe house he maintained in Saffron Hill, Clerkenwell. It was known as the Old House in West Street, and had also once been a hideaway for fellow highwaymen Jonathan Wild and Jack Sheppard.

From time to time Abershaw would keep the Bow Street Runners on their toes by working in different areas, and it was on one of these jaunts that he almost ended his career prematurely. On August 7th 1792 he was charged with attacking one William Phillip on a highway in Essex, and taking a gold watch and other belongings. How he escaped prosecution is not recorded, but eventually, after a five-year career his luck ran out.

In 1795 two Bow Street Runners, David Price and Bernard Turner, acting on a tip-off found Abershaw in the Three Brewers inn at Southwark. The highwayman tried to shoot his way out, killing Price and seriously injuring Turner who nevertheless brought Abershaw to trial and recovered.

The trial was held at Croydon assizes on July 30th 1795 and presided over by Judge Baron Pentryn. Abershaw was found guilty of murder, and when the judge put on his black cap to pronounce the death sentence the prisoner mimicked him by donning his own hat.

In his prison cell awaiting execution the highwayman asked for black cherries and used the juice to draw pictures of his escapades on the walls.

Even on the day of his execution at Kennington Common Abershaw was in high spirits. The crowd who turned out to see him was said to be large and he laughed and joked with them and kept up an 'incessant conversation' as a cart took him to the gallows.

He is said to have walked up the gallows steps with his shirt thrown open and a flower clenched in his teeth. Once there he kicked off his boots with a flourish to disprove his mother's prophecy that he would die with them on! The Times also reported that he was offered a prayer book, but threw it into the crowd.

Even after his execution the Abershaw legend continued. His body was brought back to Wimbledon to hang in chains on a gibbet that had been specially constructed on the Common overlooking his old hunting ground on the Portsmouth Road.

Contemporary reports speak of huge crowds turning out on the Sundays following to gawp at the body of the highwayman swinging in the breeze. Johnny Townsend, the famous Bow Street Runner who had organised and overseen Abershaw's execution, estimated that 100,000 people came to see the spectacle, and another source describes London as being a deserted city on the first Sunday the gibbeted body was displayed.

There was even a rumour that a plot was being hatched to cut down Abershaw's body during its first night on the gibbet and Johnny Townsend and ten of his men kept watch throughout the night, but no attempt was made to make off with the corpse.

Another story tells of an army sergeant some time later commanding his passing regiment to use the highwayman's body for target practice. He was reportedly demoted for this misdemeanour.

The Newgate Calendar also records that ruffians *procured from his decaying and piece-meal carcass the bones of his fingers and toes to convert into stoppers for their tobacco pipes'* (this has echoes of the old superstition of the Hand of Glory, when criminals would cut the hand from an executed body and attach a lock of the dead man's hair to each finger. This custom-made candelabra would then be 'blessed' by a recitation of the Lord's Prayer backwards, and once lit could be carried into a house to cast a spell on the inhabitants so they would offer no resistance to its being robbed).

After his grisly demise Jerry Abershaw was not forgotten, thanks in part to the attention of several notable writers. George Borrow included references to the highwayman in his *Romany Rye*, and on one occasion even made a pilgrimage to the Baldfaced Stag inn to see Jerry Abershaw's sword which was reputedly still there. Borrow also reveals in *Romany Rye* that he was once considering writing a biography of Jerry Abershaw, and wished that he had learned earlier of his exploits from the ostler who featured in that book. Also, in Borrow's novel *Lavengro* the ghost of Jerry Abershaw makes an appearance. You can't keep a thoroughly bad highwayman down it seems.

Local writer Captain Frederick Marryat also featured Jerry Abershaw in his book *Jacob Faithful*. When the eponymous hero of the book strays onto Wimbledon Common in a snowstorm he is startled by an 'unearthly sound' halfway between a scream and a creak. It turns out to be the body of Jerry Abershaw swinging on his gibbet. This, incidentally is supposed to be *three years* after the body was hung up.

Other writers who featured the highwayman in their work were T.G. Jackson* who included him in the *Red House*, one of the collection entitled *Six Ghost Stories*, and Bernard Cape, who featured him in the thinnest of disguises as the hero of his novel *Jemmy Abercaw*.

It is also said that Robert Louis Stevenson once planned a book about Jerry Abershaw which unfortunately never saw the light of day to join the ranks of *Kidnapped*, *Treasure Island*, and *The Strange Case of Dr. Jekyll and Mr. Hyde*.

The final seal of his immortality came when he was included in the *Dictionary of National Biography* – one of the few highwaymen to have been so honoured. The DNB noted that his name was commonly used as a synonym for a daring thief in the early 19th century.

The infamy of Abershaw is also shown by the fact that even in his own lifetime he was compared to the Prime Minister. A popular saying of the day was: 'Jerry takes purses with his pistols, and Pitt with his parliaments.' And Cyrus Redding remembers seeing a cartoon of the duel between Pitt and Tierney pinned to Abershaw's gibbet.

Even today the legend of Jerry Abershaw looms large on the Common, with Jerry's Hill, the site of his gibbeting still overlooking the old Portsmouth Road, and the silhouette sign of a highwayman at Tibbet's Corner still creaking in the breeze like his erstwhile chains.

Finally, although there is no Jerry Abershaw Arms or other inn named directly after him locally there is The Highwayman in Petersfield Rise near Putney Heath, a modern pub within a pistol's shot of his much-ridden Portsmouth Road. And apart from the Baldfaced Stag which sadly no longer exists, other local pubs claim associations with the highwayman. They include the Green Man at Putney Heath, which would certainly have been a handy local after a busy night on the roads, and the Plough at New Malden which was said to have had a secret room in which Jerry would hide when being pursued. Another of his favourites was said to be The Three Compasses at Kingston, which was in Eden Street, though in Abershaw's day it was known, perhaps more appropriately, as Heathen Street.

One thing that perhaps should be reiterated is that there never was a local highwayman named Tibbet. Because of the sign at Tibbet's Corner it is sometimes assumed that Tibbet was the name of the highwayman, but it was the name of the gate-keeper at the entrance to Lord Spencer's estate. It is thought that the similarity between the words Tibbet and gibbet has led to the confusion.

So, even after more than two hundred years Jerry's short career is far from forgotten. It still overshadows the exploits of other local highwaymen, including those even more famous who as we shall see also turned their attentions to this area.

* Famous architect and Wimbledon resident Sir Thomas Jackson published *Six Ghost Stories* in 1919 at the age of 84. This was his only work of fiction and is largely unknown today. In *The Red House*, which is set in Eagle House, Jackson's own residence, one of the characters is encouraged to commit a murder by Jerry Abershaw, whom he has met in the Baldfaced Stag inn.

RICHARD 'GALLOPING DICK' FERGUSON

Richard Ferguson came to highway robbery through the influence of Jerry Abershaw. He had been born in Hertfordshire around the same time as Abershaw was born in Kingston in the early 1770s. He worked his way up from stable boy to postilion. He found it difficult however to hold down a job due to falling in with bad company and at the age of 20 came to London.

Soon after he found work in a Piccadilly livery stable his father died and left him the not inconsiderable sum of £57. This Ferguson used to effect the life of a gentleman about town and the money was soon frittered away.

One of Ferguson's chief expenses was entertaining a prostitute named Nancy whom he had met in a Drury Lane theatre. Another of Nancy's clients at the time was one Jerry Abershaw; and although Ferguson had seen him leaving her house he was not to meet him properly until some time later.

Once Ferguson's inheritance had gone he returned to work as a postilion and it was while driving a chaise along the Great North Road that he was stopped by highwaymen.

It was a windy night and during the robbery the mask of one of the highwaymen was blown aside to reveal the face of Jerry Abershaw.

Ferguson recognised him as a client of Nancy's and Abershaw in turn realised that Ferguson knew who *he* was. Abershaw and his accomplice therefore waited for the postilion's return and met him at an inn.

Here the highwayman bribed Ferguson to join forces with them – but not as a highwayman. They asked him to supply them with information about the passengers he was carrying and more importantly the booty they took with them.

This situation suited everybody for a while but once back in the money again Ferguson returned to his dissolute ways and lost his job. It was at this point that he decided to become a highwayman himself. His riding skills were such that he earned the nickname Galloping Dick. The ostler in George Borrow's *Romany Rye* maintains that Dick was a far superior rider to Jerry Abershaw. And Dick's career as a highwayman survived for a further five years after the execution of his mentor in 1795.

Haunting the same roads as the ghost of Jerry Abershaw, Galloping Dick was not finally caught until 1800 when he was convicted of highway robbery at Aylesbury, and hanged. The 'biography' published after his execution ends with the following:

'Galloping Dick took a hasty road to perdition. Happy had it been for him had he chosen the safe path of virtue, and run a good race.'

THE GOLDEN FARMER

Disguise and subterfuge were of course essential elements in the armoury of the highwayman, but the Golden Farmer managed to successfully employ them for far longer than any other of his comrades. He managed to lead a double life as both a wealthy farmer and as a notorious highwayman for over forty years. And his secret trade bought him to Putney Heath.

Born William Davis in Wrexham in 1625 he later earned his nickname by his habit of always paying his debts in gold. He had moved to Gloucestershire as a young man and married the daughter of a wealthy innkeeper and become a farmer, so it is difficult to see why he turned to highway robbery. Perhaps it was greed, perhaps it was the pursuit of excitement, but it did not appear to be from necessity.

His wealthy father-in-law found Davis some land to farm near Bagshot and he moved there with his wife and raised 18 children. Perhaps it was this that drove him to highway robbery.

As a highwayman, the Golden Farmer, like many men of the road possessed a sharp tongue and a black sense of humour. He was also undiscriminating in his choice of victim, robbing tinkers as well as duchesses and JPs. Once, he even robbed his own landlord of the rent he had paid him shortly beforehand.

His exploits took him to various other places apart from Bagshot, and the Portsmouth Road would have been a profitable area to work.

One story tells of him robbing a grazier on Putney Heath. As he passed the old man he gave him ten guineas to look after and said that he was afraid of being robbed by three or four suspicious looking men behind him. He reasoned that they would not rob the grazier as he did not look wealthy.

The old grazier confided to the Golden Farmer that he himself had 50 guineas on him and that he would put it with that for safekeeping.

After they had ridden together for about half a mile the Golden Farmer suddenly said to the old man: 'I believe there's nobody will take the pains of robbing you or me today, therefore I think I had as good take the trouble of robbing you myself.'

The old man pleaded for mercy but the Golden Farmer cut the money from a pocket in the old man's shirt and made off with it.

He continued such ruthless robberies until he was an old man himself, and he was eventually caught in 1689 at the age of 64 after robbing a coach on the Exeter Road near Bagshot Heath. He was shot in the back by one of his victims.

He was then taken to Newgate prison and after his trial was hanged at Salisbury Court in Fleet Street on December 20th 1689. Afterwards, his body was hung in chains on the heath. It has been claimed that in the course of his career he had murdered thirteen people.

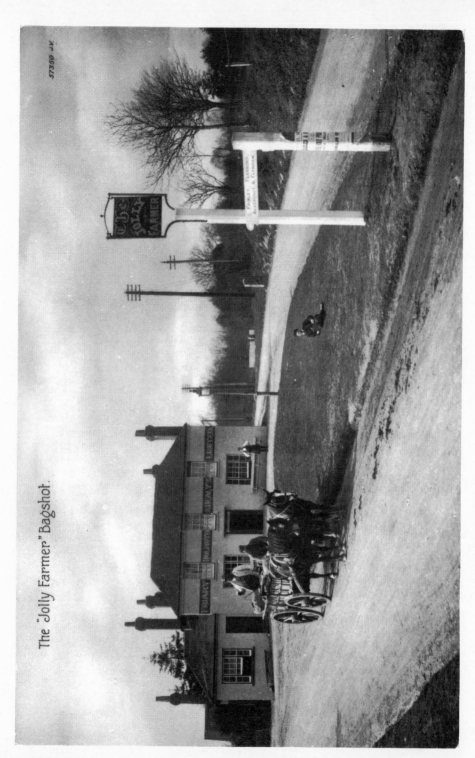

The "Jolly Farmer" Bagshot.

57350 JK

THE JOLLY FARMER (FORMERLY THE GOLDEN FARMER) c. 1905

THE GOLDEN FARMER INN

The Golden Farmer also gave his name to an inn, of which some say he was once the landlord. This seems unlikely as he was busy enough already, but other sources suggest that the inn was established in the farmhouse that once belonged to William Davis.

The first map on which the inn appears is the Senex map of 1729. It was still there almost a century later, but in 1823 the lease was transferred to another building nearby. It was at this time too that the name of the inn changed to the Jolly Farmer. It is thought that this was inspired by the cheerful expression on the face of the farmer on the inn's signboard.

The old building continued as the Golden Farmer post office for a time but was eventually pulled down in 1879 when a new post office was built at Collingwood.

Whether or not William Davis himself was the owner of the original Golden Farmer inn, it was said to be a favourite watering hole for later highwaymen such as Jerry Abershaw and Dick Turpin. It was no doubt a convenient refreshment stop after an evening's work on Bagshot Heath and its nearby coaching routes. It had too the picaresque associations of one of their more notorious brothers in crime, and the nearby gallows does not seem to have bothered them unduly.

The Jolly Farmer building is sadly no longer an inn but has recently been converted into a restaurant, so the memory of William Davis is no longer kept alive by the name. However, one mystery remains, and that is of the farmer's gold.

It is said that at the time of his arrest William Davis had still not revealed the hiding place for what must by then have been a huge stash of gold. Even his own family did not know of its whereabouts, and the secret died with the Golden Farmer.

In 1932 council workmen found part of the sandstone wall of the original inn when digging the road, and other relics of the old inn were discovered such as 18th century glasses and beer mugs and a silver-plated stirrup-iron. But the foundations of the inn were not excavated and it is here, in the cellars of the Golden Farmer that some believe the treasure still to be hidden.

OLD MOBB

An occasional partner of the Golden Farmer was Thomas Sympson, otherwise known as Old Mobb. Like the Golden Farmer he had a very lengthy career, and often robbed on the Portsmouth Road. He was hanged within six months of his old partner – on May 30th 1690 at Tyburn.

CLAUDE DUVAL

Claude Duval was probably the nearest thing to the archetypal highwayman of legend: dashing, gallant, courteous and romantic. The poet Leigh Hunt described him as *'an eternal feather in the cap of highway gentility.'* And the often sceptical highway chronicler Charles G. Harper said that he: *'ranked among his brother highwaymen as high as Rembrandt or Raphael among artists'*

The son of a miller, he was born in Normandy in 1643 and came to England at the time of the Restoration and became a footman to the Duke of Richmond.

It was not long however before he took to highway robbery and began to build the reputation of a gallant and chivalrous 'knight of the road'.

The most famous exploit that really cemented this image was when he invited one of his female victims to dance a coranto with him on the heath where he had held up her coach.

The venue for this romantic episode, if it ever happened, has never been established, and claims have variously been made for Hampstead Heath, Blackheath, Hounslow Heath, Clapham Common, and even Kent! Also, one writer has claimed that it took place on Putney Heath near to a favourite drinking place of Duval's, the Green Man. However, the same writer goes on to say that Duval was later hanged at Tibbet's Corner.

While the venue for the moonlit dance is still open to question it is certain that Duval was hanged at Tyburn – on January 21st 1670, and was buried at St. Paul's church Covent Garden.

So it looks as though this most celebrated of highwaymen may not have plied his trade locally. Though like most highwaymen, he would undoubtedly have cast his net wide to evade the authorities. So while it is not beyond the bounds of possibility that he may have carried out robberies in this area he cannot have been a regular at the Green Man as the inn was not established until around thirty years after Duval's death.

THE TWO SIDES OF THE HIGHWAYMAN

When you were held up by a highwayman you were never sure which sort you going to get. Some were violent, especially if challenged, and others were polite and even generous, though this 'generosity' was often tinged with an ironic insolence. The following local reports give a flavour of the different approaches highwaymen would take in carrying out their nefarious activities.

The Times of April 2nd 1785 reports that a Mr and Mrs Gorton of St. James's Place were stopped on their way to Streatham by two highwaymen. They took eleven guineas and two silk purses from Mr. Gorton, and then turned their attentions to his wife. She pluckily attempted to snatch the pistol that one of them was holding to her, and the highwayman, unable to extricate it, fired at her and rode off at full speed. The ball went through the woman's coat, close to her chest, and luckily passed between her and her husband. The couple were said to be greatly alarmed, each thinking the other had been shot.

The Times of September 19th 1795 reported that two or three carriages had recently been robbed near the eight-mile stone on the Croydon Road. In one of the carriages were a Mrs and Miss Lewis and their maid-servant. The villains fired one pistol at the coachman and another one into the carriage. The coachman took the ball in his side, and the maid-servant was shot through the hand and was predicted to lose two fingers due to the injury.

But sometimes the highwaymen came off worst in these desperate struggles. On August 31st 1786 the Times reported that a gentleman and lady returning to town from Kingston in a post chaise were attacked near the foot of Kingston Hill by two highwaymen. The gentleman, having pistols with him fired and wounded one of them and the other one was later taken into custody. One of them was found to be in possession of a brass-barrelled pistol loaded with large shot.

In August 1785 a Mr Jonathan Burnet and his daughter were going into town from Guildford in a post-chaise when they were stopped on Putney Heath by a highwayman. He robbed Mr Burnet of his purse which contained five guineas and some silver, and then robbed the daughter of her purse containing half a guinea and seven shillings. He then tipped the coach driver half a crown and told him to go on.

The Times of September 19th 1795 reports that a Mr Baxter of Gray's Inn and another gentleman were returning to town from Richmond when they were stopped on Putney Common by two highwaymen. They took their watches and seven and a half guineas in gold and eleven shillings in silver. They then rode off, but not before wishing the two gentlemen a good night. The highwaymen were described as being young and polite and well-mounted on bay horses.

On April 13th the same year the Times reported that a Mr J. Hamet had been attacked by three footpads near the nine-mile stone on Kingston Road. They robbed him of whatever money he had on him and advised that if he should be held up by any other robbers on his journey that he should say he had 'been spoke to'.

WILLIAM GETTINGS

Gettings came to London in 1707 at the age of 16 and after a short apprenticeship in shoplifting and housebreaking became a fully-fledged highwayman.

Many of his exploits took place in south London and on one occasion he held up the stagecoach of Squire Dashwood on Putney Heath, taking gold and silver and a gold watch.

In nearby Tooting he noticed a nobleman walking in his own private gardens and gave him the impression that he too was a gentleman and wished to view the gardens. Taken into his confidence the nobleman showed him around, only for Gettings to suddenly produce a pistol and demand his money, watch and diamond ring. He then tied up his victim and escaped.

He eventually received his comeuppance however, and was hanged at Tyburn on September 25th 1713.

WILLIAM JOYCE

This highwayman held up one John Hicks on Putney Heath but was surprised when his victim gamely fought back. The men had fired shots at one another but had not come to any harm. Joyce was so impressed with the courage of Hicks that he invited him for a drink in Putney. The Green Man was not in existence at this time in the late 17th century so it may have been one of the several pubs in the town.

The two men reportedly spent an hour or two regaling each other with stories before Joyce left, presenting Hicks with five guineas before he did so. Perhaps the only case of a victim being better off after an encounter with a highwayman!

Joyce, incidentally, ended his life in the time-honoured tradition of gentlemen of the road. He was hanged in July 1696.

CAPTAIN EVAN EVANS

Evans had the benefit of a good education and the beginnings of a career in law. It is said however that in his dealings with crooks and highway robbers he fell into their ways – perhaps seeing the easy money that could be made. Although born in Wales he came south-east and carried out many of his attacks on the Portsmouth Road.

He and his brother once encountered some constables commanding a group of about 30 men who were being press-ganged into service at Portsmouth. The two highwaymen attacked the constables and took their money before setting the unwilling conscripts free.

Captain Evans and his brother were eventually arrested for a highway robbery committed in Barnet and were hanged at Hertford in 1708. The Captain was 29 years old, and his brother was 23.

THOMAS ROWLAND

Rowland was original if nothing else – he committed his robberies dressed as a woman. With the aid of this disguise he managed a career of 18 years and reputedly robbed on the Portsmouth Road by Wimbledon Common and Putney Heath as well as Clapham Common and other nearby spots.

He was born in 1659 at Ware in Hertfordshire and began his career in villainy by stealing a horse from the Duke of Beaufort. He later came to London and began his lengthy stint as a highwayman. Once a robbery was committed he would ride away side-saddle looking like an innocent woman.

He was eventually caught after robbing someone of £1200 worth of bone lace on Hounslow Heath. He was hanged at Tyburn on October 24th 1699.

TOM WATERS

The old Portsmouth Road with its regular coaches and lonely heath land seemed to be a magnet for highwaymen, and amongst others it drew Tom Waters to its windswept wastes.

Waters was born in Henley-on-Thames in 1665 not a tremendous distance from his future hunting grounds on the coaching route. He was an egalitarian highwayman, robbing both rich and poor alike. He once robbed a band of gypsies not far from Walton and on another occasion held up the admiral of the English fleet, Sir Ralph Delaval. This attack took place on the Portsmouth Road and netted the highwayman ten guineas.

He had asked the admiral about his beliefs and the admiral angrily demanded to know what his beliefs had to do with him. Waters then asked if he believed he would be robbed before the end of the day, and when the admiral answered no, produced his pistols and took his money.

Again ringing the changes Waters held up near Guildford a woman believed to be a witch. Ignoring her curses he took her purse, but not long afterwards was caught and hanged at Tyburn on July 17th 1691. Perhaps the woman was a witch and had successfully cursed him after all.

Preparing for the journey.

1. The traveller. 2. The highwayman. 3. The breakdown. 4 and 5. "Your money or your life!" 6. The end of the journey. 7. Appendix.

FROM START TO FINISH—A TALE OF THE ROAD.

THE GALLOWS AND THE GIBBET

Considering how many highwaymen ended their days on the gallows it is surprising that the prospect did not keep more of them from their lives of crime. But, if anything, their final trip to the 'three-legged mare' seemed to have been almost a celebratory event, adding the final touch to their contrived notoriety.

Although many highwaymen were hanged at Tyburn (near present day Marble Arch), there were other gallows more locally.

Jerry Abershaw of course was hanged at Kennington Common, but others, such as Nicholas Wells were 'turned off' at Kingston. The exact location of this place of execution remains cloaked in mystery. Indeed, there is very little surviving information about it at all.

The consensus seems to be that the gallows stood at what is now Kingsnympton estate. It is also possible that it may not have been in exactly the same spot throughout its history as different maps show different locations. The map made for Charles I at the time of the enclosure of Richmond Park shows the gallows at Kingston Common near the park boundary (there is also a 'Gibbet Close' nearby). But it seems to have gone by the 19th century, and perhaps earlier, otherwise would it not have been a fitting place for Abershaw to have been hanged in 1795?

There was also a gallows at Croydon in the 17th century. Charles G. Harper writes of a *'startlingly large gallows, like a football goal'* a mile and a half from the London side of Croydon. It was featured in Ogilby's Britannia in 1675.

Also south of the Thames, at Southwark was the Horsemongers Prison and scaffold which was said to have had as many important executions as Newgate.

The highwayman's last journey to the 'hanging tree' by all accounts took on something of a carnival atmosphere, attracting all sections of society. There were often large crowds, the taverns would open early, and there would be men selling pies and gingerbread, women selling fruit from baskets at the foot of the scaffold, and others hawking the latest cheaply printed broadsheets detailing the life and crimes of the condemned. And as the cart took the victims to the gallows it made a customary stop at an alehouse for them to partake of a final drink.

At Tyburn there was even a permanently fixed 'grandstand' of seats for which the better-off could pay half a crown to witness an execution.

The entire proceedings were an event from start to finish and were drenched in tradition, folklore and superstition. Some believed that the hands of the hanged man had healing properties, and they would touch them to cure anything from warts to tumours.

It was also believed that a storm on the day of an execution signified the innocence of the person about to be hanged. At an execution on Kennington Common in 1763 the crowd attempted to free the condemned man after a storm broke out and the military were called in to prevent the rescue.

Hangings in London and the surrounding area peaked in the 1780s. The number of executions ordered by the Old Bailey from 1781-1785 was 293, but by contrast the figure for the first five years of the 19th century was just 43. This decline also ties in with the number of reported highway robberies (see End of an Era).

While many highwaymen went to the gallows with gay abandon and seemed to relish the final bow with which they left the stage of notoriety they seemed to have very different views about the practice of gibbeting. This public display of the body of a hanged man was feared by many more than the tightening of the 'hempen cravat' on the 'nibbing chit'. It is not known why highwaymen feared the gibbet more than the scaffold, but perhaps it was the belief that they would not be able to rest in peace while their bodies remained unburied.

An ancient practice, gibbeting was revived in 1752 when the Murder Act allowed judges to impose it as part of sentencing. It was seen as a graphic warning to others not to follow the path of crime that had been taken by the gibbeting victim. The bodies of the criminals were usually hung in chains or encased in a kind of metal cage. They were often also covered in pitch which acted as a preservative. Presumably the longer the body stayed on public view, the greater its deterrent effect.

Gibbeting was often used for highwaymen convicted of robbing mail coaches, and two brothers, William and Robert Drewett were thus punished for robbing the Portsmouth mail at Midhurst in 1799.

The practice of gibbeting lasted for eighty years, but as the 19th century went on there was a growing distaste for it, at least among some of the populace. But although objections were raised by many there was still a crowd of twenty thousand people to watch the last gibbeting in 1832 of murderer James Cook in Leicestershire. The practice was officially ended in 1834.

But at its height a public gibbeting was a huge attraction. When Jerry Abershaw was gibbeted on Putney Heath in 1795 the crowd was estimated to be 100,000 and the trip to see him hanging in chains was said to be a 'favourite Sunday outing' for months afterwards.

CAPTAIN DUDLEY

This army captain had been stationed in Tangiers but on his return to England fell on hard times and took to highway robbery. He robbed on the Portsmouth Road among others and was known to be something of a Robin Hood, often giving some of his ill-gotten booty to the poor.

On one occasion he even robbed the keeper of Newgate prison which must have been a particular pleasure for one whose many confederates had been incarcerated there.

Dudley was finally caught attempting to rob the Duke of Lauderdale on Hounslow Heath. He was hanged at Tyburn on February 22nd 1681.

NICHOLAS WELLS

Wells was, like Dick Turpin, a butcher by trade. Born in Penshurst, Kent, in 1684, he later lived in East Grinstead and worked in Southwark. A failed marriage left him in financial difficulties and he resorted to theft and highway robbery.

He once robbed Robert Fielding on Putney Heath. Fielding, sometimes known as Beau Fielding due to his amorous exploits was knocked off his horse by Wells and then tied up. The highwayman took 20 guineas from him and left him to extricate himself.

Apart from highway robbery Nicholas Wells was also known for one other curious incident. Captain Alexander Smith relates how Wells exchanged his wife for a jackdaw with footpad William Maw. The contract they drew up was as follows:

We, the subscribers, William Maw of London, joiner and Nicholas Wells of Penshurst in the county of Kent, butcher, each of us being burdened with a useless moveable, the former with a jackdaw and the latter with a wife, declare that we have thought fit, for the convenience of one another, out of our own pure and free will to make a barter and truck of the jackdaw for the wife; yielding up, the one to the other, all right and title that we have to the said wife and jackdaw and quitting forever all claim to them, without any manner of complaint or demand hereafter to the premises so trucked. To which bargain and agreement in token of hearty consent and satisfaction, we have hereunto set our hands and seals. Dated at Deptford on the 10th of May 1710.

Unlike many other local highwaymen Wells was not hanged at Tyburn. He ended his days on the scaffold at Kingston. He was arrested after robbing fellow butcher James Wilmot at Epsom and hanged an March 28th 1712.

THE SKATING HIGHWAYMAN

Now here is a true original, Jonathan Simpson, who was known as the Skating Highwayman. In the early weeks of 1683 London was in the icy grip of the Great Frost. The River Thames froze over and the ice was eighteen inches thick.

Simpson, nothing if not an opportunist, equipped himself with a pair of skates and thus committed many robberies on the river between Fulham and Kingston bridges. There were probably good pickings to be had too as the Frost Fair had become a popular attraction, with members of the nobility and even Charles II paying a visit to the frozen river.

Once the Great Frost was over Simpson had to revert to horseback robberies and targeted the Portsmouth Road. He himself was conned when a victim handed over a purseful of coins only for Simpson to later discover that they were gaming counters.

He is said to have kept the purse until he could hold up the same victim again and give it back in person. When he did he demanded that the man hand over his breeches this time so that he could search them later at his leisure.

Simpson was finally caught for robbing two army captains in Acton. He was hanged at Tyburn on September 8th 1686 at the age of 32.

THE HIGHWAYMAN PARSON

Highwaymen, it seems come from all walks of life including that of the church. In the 17th century Parson Darby made extra cash by robbing on Bagshot Heath, not far from the home of Golden Farmer William Davis.

Darby was eventually found out by his stableman who grew suspicious that the parson's horse seemed to have frequently been used during the night. But by this time Darby had shot dead the driver of a mailcoach who had attempted to flee from the robber.

Today, the place name Darby Green near Camberley remains a reminder of this notorious highwayman.

THE GETAWAY

ROBBING THE 'NOBS'

Many highwaymen were not too fussy about whom they robbed, whether they were tinkers or tradesmen, and these were clearly the softer targets. But the more ambitious and daring robbers were after the big money and this of course meant robbing the nobility. The risks were greater, but so were the rewards. A few local examples of the rich and influential being robbed follow:

On June 21st 1794 Lord Mulgrave was crossing Putney Common in his post-chaise on his way to Portsmouth when he was attacked by three highwaymen. The Times reports that:

'The noble lord would not be robbed, and the ruffians instantly fired into the carriage. One of the lamps was struck off by a shot and a ball went through the back of the chaise close to his lordship's head. Lord Mulgrave fired two pistols and one of the men dropt, but recovered and rode off and was followed by his companions.'

On December 19th 1794 Captain Burton of the navy was held up in his post-chaise at the top of Kingston Hill. Three footpads escaped with his watch and £26.

On January 11th 1795 Colonel Paris, (a French gentleman, we are told!) was travelling to Roehampton along Kingston Road with an English lady companion when his post-chaise was stopped by two footpads. He opened the window of his carriage, and seeing one of the robbers approach with a pistol, fired at him. The footpad fell and his companion, who had been pointing his pistol at the postilion, then fired at Colonel Paris. He missed, and the postilion took the chance to speed the carriage away from the robbers.

Lord Onslow seems to have been particularly unlucky with highwaymen. He was held up on Wimbledon Common in the late 18th century (see 'A Miscellany of Highwaymen' chapter), and on November 21st 1799 was robbed on Barnes Common. Two highwaymen, with crape masks over their faces demanded his watch and money. Lord Onslow gave them a guinea and a half, but did not have his watch. The robbers noticed that the Lord's servant was attempting to conceal his own watch and they demanded it. Lord Onslow ordered the servant to hand it over, but inexplicably the highwaymen handed it back *'with civility'*.

Within a week of this incident Lord Onslow established patrols of his cavalry regiment to scour the Richmond area where they were quartered to root out any highwaymen. The Times commented that: *'the numerous robbers who infest every avenue to the metropolis and plunder before the multitude in the broad face of day is most discreditable to our police.'*

On November 26th, a few days after the attack on Lord Onslow, the Imperial Minister Count Stahremberg was held up between East Sheen and Richmond. Two highwaymen stopped the coach carrying the Count, his wife, and Lady Clarges and took *'some guineas.'*

So even fifty years after the Bow Street Runners had been formed in 1749 the nobility were more or less having to fend for themselves in the face of highway robbery.

JAMES MACLAINE

James Maclaine was often referred to as the Gentleman Highwayman, but as with many of his trade the outward appearance of gentility was an affectation. He was the son of a Presbytarian minister but had only achieved the station of a simple butler before his highway robbery career began.

One local incident that amusingly illustrates the social complexities of mid-18th century England concerns an argument Maclaine had at Putney Bowling Club.

The bowling green had been established in the 1630s and became a fashionable meeting place which survived for almost a century and a half, attracting the upper echelons of society and of course aspiring 'gentlemen' such as Maclaine.

An army officer at the club had cast doubt on Maclaine's claims to gentility and he in turn challenged the officer to a duel. The officer however refused to draw pistols with Maclaine unless he could prove his noble birth in writing! To be shot in a duel would be bad enough, but to be shot by a member of the lower orders would be perhaps too much to bear.

Maclaine's highway robbery activities took place in local areas such as Richmond, but perhaps his most notorious robbery was that of Horace Walpole, son of Sir Robert Walpole, in Hyde Park. Following the robbery Maclaine seems to have been overcome with contrition and in keeping with his nickname wrote two letters of apology to Walpole.

Like so many other highwaymen Maclaine ended his life on the gallows at Tyburn – on October 3rd 1750 at the age of 36.

The post was a favourite target of highwaymen as this local incident illustrates: on February 25th 1785 between 4 and 5 a.m. the post boy bringing the southern mail from Kingston was stopped near the Baldfaced Stag inn on the Portsmouth Road at the edge of Wimbledon Common. Two footpads broke open the cart and took the mailbags. It is surprising what a wide area the mail came from. It included bags from Portsmouth, Petersfield, Chichester, Arundel, Guildford, Godalming, Haslemere, Midhurst, Ripley, Petworth, Kingston, Esher, Farnham and Cobham.

EDWARD HINTON

Edward Hinton is probably the only highwayman to have escaped the gallows twice – although he was not so lucky the third time.

Born in 1673, he had become a highwayman at a young age and was caught and sentenced to death before he was 20. He was pardoned however, because of his youth and the good family from which he came.

But foolishly, he continued with highway robbery in Surrey and Middlesex and was caught on a second occasion. This time he was transported, but he managed to stir up a mutiny on the ship and escaped to Portsmouth with several other criminals.

Back in England he returned to his chosen profession and a story survives of one encounter on Putney Heath which shows that he did have some redeeming features.

He and an accomplice stopped a coach one night and found the occupants to be a clergyman and his daughter. The clergyman pleaded for their mercy and the highwayman said: *'All we desire is your blessing and a kiss from your pretty daughter.'*

Despite the father's protests the highwaymen each kissed the girl and rode off without robbing them.

It was not long after this that Hinton gave up highway robbery, but unable to lead an honest life he was eventually caught robbing a house and was hanged at Tyburn.

Even once the Bow Street Runners were in operation they were not always in the right place at the right time as the following story shows: on November 10th 1798 a Mr Hick and his wife and child were held up in their post-chaise near Croydon. They were attacked and robbed by five footpads armed with knives and bludgeons. It was reported that the Bow Street Runners were on duty that night, but instead of being on the road they were drinking at the King's Arms inn.

WILLIAM PAGE – WITH PHAETON NEARBY

WILLIAM PAGE

It is not known how many highwaymen used the excuse of an unhappy childhood to account for their criminality but William Page certainly had one.

He was born in 1730, the son of a bargeman at Hampton. When Page was just ten his father drowned at Putney and his mother resorted to making a modest living selling herbal remedies.

After a succession of jobs as a young adult William Page took to the road to fund his appetite for gambling and expensive clothes. He was so hard up when he commenced his career as a highwayman that he committed his first robbery (on the Highgate coach) with a pair of borrowed pistols and a hired horse.

As his career progressed Page developed an ingenious strategy of his own. Dressed as a gentleman he would drive to a secluded spot in a phaeton (open-topped carriage) and then change into old clothes and a wig. He would then ride one of the horses to a convenient place nearby and hold up a coach before going back to the phaeton and changing back into his finery. He would then drive home looking to the outside world like a gentleman and arousing no suspicions about his nefarious activities.

This tactic however was undermined on one occasion when some farmhands on Putney Heath found the phaeton and a single horse and made off with them. But William Page's ingenuity saved the situation when he found the phaeton parked outside an inn.

Removing his outer clothes and throwing them down a well Page ran into the inn and said that the farmhands had stripped and robbed him. The story was believed and the alleged miscreants were arrested. With perhaps some notion of honour among thieves however, Page refused to give evidence against them and they were later released.

Page continued his career for another three years, even surviving arrest and cross-examination by noted Justice of the Peace (and novelist) Henry Fielding, and later, a bullet wound from one of his victims.

Eventually though, he was arrested for robbing a Captain Farrington, and one of his accomplices, John Darwell, turned evidence against him.

Page was hanged on Penenden Heath on April 6th 1758.

DICK TURPIN

So, did the legendary Dick Turpin ever rob coaches in these parts? The stories of all highwaymen swirl in a cloud of legend, fantasy, romance and fancy, but none more so than that of Dick Turpin.

He has become the best-known of all highwaymen with his legendary ride to York on Black Bess the most celebrated of all his daring deeds. But that ride was never made, at least, not by Turpin, and probably not on a horse named Black Bess.

There is no doubt that Turpin was a notorious highwayman in his time, though he was a ruffian and a bully rather than the dashing cavalier type of legend. On more than one occasion during a house break-in he threatened to sit his victims on their own blazing fires if they would not co-operate. So how did he gain his legendary reputation?

Largely it seems from *Rookwood*, a fictionalised account of his life written by Harrison Ainsworth in 1834. It is here that the ride to York (actually achieved by highwayman John Nevison), was first attributed to Dick Turpin.

Probably the most surprising fact about Dick Turpin's career as a highwayman was how remarkably brief it was – just over two years.

Richard Turpin, who was born in Hemel hempstead in 1705 started his working life as a butcher, and by the age of 21 had his own shop. This enterprise was not however as honest as it may sound – he ensured a regular supply of fresh meat by stealing sheep.

When the source of his meat was discovered Turpin fled and for a while tried his hand at smuggling. From this he progressed to housebreaking, and joined the notorious Essex-based Gregory gang, who themselves had started as deer stealers.

This vicious band of criminals broke into houses in and around London and thought nothing of attacking their victims in the course of a robbery.

One report, from 1735 has them pillaging the house of a Mr Sheldon near Croydon Church. They bound and gagged the coachman in the stable, and when the owner came to investigate, forced him to guide them to all the valuables in the house. They also stole eleven guineas, and in an uncharacteristic show of compassion, gave two guineas back. They then audaciously went to a nearby tavern, the Half Moon, for a drink.

But their brutal career was not to last much longer. On February 7th 1735 they robbed a farmer, Mr Francis of Marylebone, and even beat his daughter and maid during the robbery. A £100 reward was offered for their capture and two of the gang were caught and hanged on the evidence of a third.

It was at this point that Turpin began his career as a highwayman, and one of his accomplices, Rowden the Pewterer, was a survivor of the Gregory gang. It is also at this point that the legendary highwayman turned his attentions to these parts.

A newspaper reports that on July 10th 1735 about 8.00 p.m. two gentlemen were robbed between Wandsworth and Barnes Commons by: *'two highwaymen, supposed to be Turpin the Butcher and Rowden the Pewterer, the remaining two of Gregory's Gang, who robbed them of their money and dismounted them; made them pull off their horse's bridles, then turning them loose, they rode off towards Roehampton where a gentleman was robbed (as supposed by the same highwaymen), of a watch and £4 in money.'*

Two weeks later, on July 24th, the Grub Street Journal reports: *'On Monday, Mr Omar, of Southwark, meeting between Barnes Common and Wandsworth, Turpin the Butcher, with another person, clapt spurs to his horse, but they coming up with him obliged him to dismount and Turpin, suspecting that he knew him, would have shot him but was prevented by the other who pulled the pistol out of his hand.'*

Also around this time there is the following report: *'A Reverend Amey, a country clergyman who lodges at the Star inn near the Strand'* being robbed two miles from the London side of Richmond of: *'his silver watch, four guineas, and some silver, by two highwaymen, well-mounted and well-dressed. The rogues turned his horse loose and went off towards Richmond.'*

And on Sunday August 16th Turpin and Rowden are found on what was to become Jerry Abershaw's home territory 60 years later, the Portsmouth Road between Putney and Kingston Hill. The Grub Street Journal reports that they robbed: *'several gentlemen on horseback or in coaches.'*

This local flurry of activity was not to last however, and perhaps not wishing to push their luck for too long in one area, the pair moved on to Blackheath.

By June 1737 Dick Turpin had a price of £200 on his head and again fled London, this time for Yorkshire, his career as a highwayman over. This career, which has become celebrated in legend had lasted a little over two years. Rowden the Pewterer was caught in July 1737 and transported.

In Yorkshire Turpin effected the outward appearance of a gentleman but was unable to stay honest and took to stealing horses. He had now come almost full-circle from the sheep-stealing of his youth, and it was for horse-stealing ironically that he was eventually convicted. He had evaded arrest for smuggling, violent housebreaking, and highway robbery but went to the gallows on April 7th 1739 for this relatively petty offence.

But whatever the truth may have been, the legend of Dick Turpin is as potent as ever, and at the height of his colourful career he was certainly active in the local roads and commons that surround us today.

A MISCELLANY OF HIGHWAYMEN

Apart from those mentioned in the preceding pages, there were many other highwaymen working the roads and commons locally, many of who retain their anonymity when featuring in newspaper reports. Some others seem to have been so active in so many areas that a mere passing mention of them is all we have locally. Here is a small selection of these miscellaneous highwaymen:

Peter Finloryer was an extremely busy highwayman who not only committed robberies on Putney Heath, Barnes Common and Wandsworth Common, but also managed to fit in Romford, Kensington, Dartford, Finchley and Hounslow, among others. He was hanged in 1750.

Thomas Banks was hanged at Kingston for highway robbery in 1777, but little is known of his specific crimes. The fact that he was hanged here rather than at Tyburn may indicate that his crimes were local too.

One tale, of an anonymous highwayman gives the lie to the idea that Jerry Abershaw was the last of the highwaymen. It also shows that the gallant highwayman of legend did exist after all, and almost right to the end of the highway robbery era. The Morning Chronicle of January 14th 1797 reports:

'A very gallant highway robbery was lately committed on Wimbledon Common upon the person of a young married lady. After receiving her purse, the robber politely demanded an elegant ring which he discovered on her finger. This she peremptorily refused, saying she "would sooner part with her life"; the hero of the turf rejoined: "Since you value the ring so much madam, allow me the honour of saluting the fair hand which wears it, and I shall deem it a full equivalent!" The hand was instantly stretched through the chariot window , and the kiss being received, the highwayman thanked her for her condescension, and instantly galloped off perfectly satisfied with the commutation.'

Talk of highway robberies often conjures up images of moonlit encounters on lonely roads, but one local incident shows that audacious highwaymen were just as likely to commit their robberies in daylight, and in full view of others. A writer in Sharpe's London Magazine recalls in 1846:

'Some fifty years ago I unconsciously witnessed from the drawing room window of a friend's house in Wimbledon a highway robbery, committed in open day on the late Lord Onslow. About eleven o'clock on one fine morning in the Summer, I saw his lordship's carriage stopped by two highwaymen on horseback, within the sight and call of several labourers who were at work in the adjoining field, and who, like me, must have believed it impossible that a robbery should be committed in a public place, and at such an hour. No doubt they thought, as did I, that the young man in the red jacket who was at the window of the chariot was the post boy with Lord Onslow's letters. In this case the highwaymen owed their safety and impunity to their hardihood, and to the good generalship which led them to effect their retreat easily from the apparent impossibility of the undertaking.'

THE PORTSMOUTH ROAD

Much of the activity of our local highwaymen took place as we have seen, on the old Portsmouth Road, which was a major coaching route in the 18th and 19th centuries.

Coaches would leave Piccadilly and travel down through London and over Putney bridge (built 1729), then on through Putney Heath, Wimbledon Common and Kingston, to Portsmouth – a journey of over seventy miles. For anyone travelling the entire distance there would be several stops at inns along the way to change horses, obtain refreshment and stop overnight.

Passengers travelled in constant fear of attack by highwaymen and often kept their valuables in their boots or in the lining of their hats.

The sight of erstwhile highwaymen hanging from gibbets along the route at Putney Heath, Hindhead and other spots may have been of some comfort to travellers but it did not seem to have deterred the highwaymen. At Kingston too was the gallows on which many a highwayman ended his days, but still the robberies continued.

Stagecoach travel was by all accounts a hazardous enough mode of transport without the highwaymen. The roads were unmade, rough and pitted, with the rain making them boggy and the lack of rain causing dust to be thrown up into the carriage. The carriages were often cramped and uncomfortable, and the complete overturn of a coach on a sharp bend was not unheard of.

The overnight stops at inns were often far from luxurious, and would give opportunistic highwaymen the chance to assess the potential wealth of the travellers who stayed there. It was often contended too that many landlords of inns were in collusion with highwaymen, and there was obviously a great temptation for unscrupulous innkeepers to exploit their position.

We know that Jerry Abershaw based himself at the Baldfaced Stag and that the Green Man on Putney Heath was a favourite with highwaymen and footpads alike. Several pubs in Kingston, such as the Three Compasses, also claim associations with highwaymen, and the aptly named Robin Hood in Kingston Vale was a regular stopping point for the Portsmouth coach.

The road was also a major mail-coach route, and the Portsmouth mail was frequently held up by highwaymen.

With its lonely stretches of heath land and many coaching inns the Portsmouth Road remained a favourite with highwaymen as long as they continued to flourish, and even today their ghosts and legends cling to their old hunting ground. On a misty November night the commons and heath along this road can still conjure up the atmosphere of the age of highway robbery.

FOOTPADS

A note must be made too of the footpads, the pedestrian poor relations of the mounted highwaymen. Their stories have neither been so well documented as those of the highwaymen, nor have any of them joined Turpin, Duval and others in legend and popular folklore.

They were a lowly breed, preying on easy targets perhaps no less poor than themselves. Some reports of footpad robberies have been included in the preceding pages, but in some reports the term 'footpad' seems to have been wrongly used. A robbery is described, and then we are told how the 'footpads' escaped on horseback!

Two local footpads, Witlock and Brown however have been remembered and even achieved the dubious distinction of being hanged at Tyburn.

Joseph Witlock and William Brown favoured the area between Putney Heath and Kingston and their speciality was to earmark a potential victim in a tavern or inn and then follow and attack him as he made his way home. And if their victims were slightly the worse for drink then that was probably a factor that made their job easier.

One night they spotted two potential victims in the Green Man at Putney Heath and lay in wait for them as they left the inn. They tied their hands behind their backs and secured twenty guineas as well as pocket-knives and tobacco boxes. Not content with this the cowardly pair then attacked a baker's boy and extracted a few pennies and a silver buckle from him.

Despite the relatively petty nature of their crimes they were hanged at Tyburn in 1773. (Incidentally, the year that Jerry Abershaw was born).

A footpad listens for footsteps

END OF AN ERA

On paper, the end of the highway robbery era looks abrupt, and almost too neat. The reports of highway robberies reduce dramatically right at the close of the 18th century. In practice the robberies no doubt continued to some extent, as the occasional report still appears as late as the middle of the 19th century. Perhaps the newspapers had grown tired of reporting the familiar details of post-chaises being stopped by men with crape masks over their faces. Certainly, there were general despairing comments in the newspapers about the frequency of such attacks. As late as December 17th 1798 the Times comments:

'The uncommon number of highway robberies call loudly for the interposition of the police. Why may not the cavalry, in the neighbourhood of barracks and quarters, patrol the roads at a certain distance, and on certain hours? What more terrible enemy have we than our own banditti from which they can protect us? The whole circle about Croydon has offered to raise a subscription for the above purpose but the Commanding Officer has put his decided negative upon it.'

Lord Onslow, as we have seen did implement something along these lines in the Richmond area.

And exactly a year later, on December 17th 1799 the Times said that: *'Robberies in the vicinity of London are becoming daily more audacious'.*

But then, after a spate of highway robberies in 1800, the number suddenly decreases from 1801 onwards. Locally, we find a highway robbery on Putney Common in December 1801, one on Wimbledon Common and one in Wandsworth in 1802, then nothing else until October 1807 when one is committed on Putney Common. Thereafter the attacks are few and far between and gradually peter out altogether.

So why did the highway robbery era end so suddenly? It was probably a combination of reasons. Writer George Borrow suggested three: the enclosure of common and heath land, the refusal of magistrates to grant licences to inns that harboured highwaymen, and the mounted patrols which were established in London. To this we can add the fact that the nobility at least were now arming themselves before travelling and were prepared to fight back, and the reduced need for people to carry large sums of money due to bank cheques being introduced in 1760. Also, in the next century came the innovation of railway travel.

Strangely, the threat of the gallows though does not seem to have bothered would-be highwaymen unduly. At a time when Kennington Common was being regularly used as a place of execution it was also a notorious spot for highway robbery. And one report in November 1800 tells us of the Portsmouth coach being held up within sight of Jerry Abershaw's gibbet on Putney Heath.

Perhaps there was also something of a new century ushering in new ways, and certainly, as the 19th century went on railway travel became established and coach travel was used less. Other changes, such as the establishment of a regular police force in 1829 also contributed. (The Bow Street Runners had been in existence since 1749).

So an era had ended, and however brutal and frightening some of the encounters had been to those robbed the Golden Age of the highwayman seems to have added some colour and excitement to those times, and not just when viewed through the distorting mirror of time. Even in the midst of that era there were some, such as the society ladies who wept at the funeral of Claude Duval, and the crowd who enjoyed a joke with Jerry Abershaw as he rode to the gallows, who revelled in the romance and rebelliousness of these gentlemen of the road.

And perhaps nothing shows better the extraordinary wish to romanticise the lives of the highwaymen than the huge reputation built round Dick Turpin whose career as a highwayman, as we have seen, lasted a mere two years.

THE LANGUAGE OF HIGHWAYMEN

Highwaymen, footpads and other criminals of the 18th century developed a language all their own. Partly to converse with one another without outsiders understanding, and partly perhaps as any 'profession' has its own jargon.

Whenever highwaymen have been directly quoted their language has been very colourful, and although some of the slang is still with us today (such as 'flog', meaning to whip), much of it has disappeared over the centuries. The following few phrases give some idea of the phraseology employed by these 'knights of the road'.

As many highwaymen ended up on the gallows, it is perhaps not surprising that they coined many euphemisms for it. Among them are 'the three-legged mare', 'three-legged stool', 'nubbing chit', 'Tyburn tree', and 'deadly never-green'. Phrases for being hanged include 'wearing the hempen cravat', to 'go west', and 'cry cockles'.

General phrases include:

Ratler – a coach
Ratling cove – coach driver
Cull – a foolish man/victim
Darkmans – night
Ken – house
Boozing Ken – an inn
Prancer – horse
Nim – steal (nim the nab = steal the hat)
Nubbing cove – the hangman
Bilk – rob
Nut crackers – the pillory
Rum padders – highwaymen
Whit – Newgate prison
Bowsy – drunk
Focus – tobacco
Joseph - cloak
Queer cuffin – justice of the peace
Tip me my snack – give me my share
Mill the gig with your Betty – break open the door with your crowbar
Ding the cull on the poll – knock the man on the head
Halt for the cull are leery – stop because they suspect us
Draw your tail – draw your sword
Bite the bill from the cull – take your victim's sword
Bite the wiper – steal the handkerchief
Nim the crap – steal the money
The child of darkmans – the bellman
Dub the gigger – open the door
Fib the cove for the lowr in his bung – beat the man for the money in his purse
Flick the Peter – cut off the (victim's) cloak
Rum glaziers – good eyes
Stow your whids and plant 'em – be careful what you say

ACKNOWLEDGEMENTS

Ruth Murphy

Wandsworth Local Studies Centre

Surrey Record Office

Surrey Heath Museum

Special thanks to Charles Toase for his generous sharing of sources

PHOTOGRAPHS/PICTURES

Jerry Abershaw (P.8) – Richard Milward

Jerry Abershaw (P.12) – John O' London magazine

William Page – Wandsworth Local Studies Centre

Others – Author's own collection

SELECT BIBLIOGRAPHY

A History of the Lives and Robberies of the Most Notorious Highwaymen – Captain Alexander Smith

Half Hours with the Highwaymen – Charles G. Harper

Stand and Deliver – Patrick Pringle

Highwayman's Heath – Gordon Maxwell

The Hanging Tree – V.A.C. Gatrell

Golden Farmer – George C.B. Poulter